Drawings of
Old Boston Houses

Drawings of Old Boston Houses

and Nearby Areas on Cape Cod and the North Shore

Janet Doub Erickson

Abt Books • Cambridge, Massachusetts

I am grateful to my friend Clark Abt, an unusually imaginative publishing entrepreneur among other things, whose suggestion one summer afternoon in Wellfleet started my search through old portfolios for drawings of this city we both love; to Kay Hardy, Vicki Levin, and Sally MacGillivray, whose editorial support at Abt Books helped organize the material; and to my husband Eric and sons Joel and Andrew who found the missing originals. I know I made more drawings of Boston, and I wish I could locate them to fill the gaps in this memoir of the city that I used to know.

Library of Congress Cataloging-in-Publication Data
Erickson, Janet Doub
Drawings of Old Boston Houses and nearby areas on Cape Cod and the North Shore
1. Erickson, Janet Doub. 2. Boston Region (Mass.) in art. 3. Cape Cod (Mass.) in art. 4. Dwellings in art. I. Title.
NC139.E75A4 1989   741.93 — dc19
ISBN 0-89011-597-4   ISBN 0-89011-598-2 (pbk.)

Printed in the United States of America

This collection of drawings is dedicated to all my children,
Joel, Sally, Eva, Andrew and Lars Erickson, even though they
were not in the picture when most of these were made.

Part I   A City Upon a Hill

Drawings and Dimensions (WIDTH AND HEIGHT IN INCHES)

Frontispiece	Longwood Avenue near Brookline Avenue	*(20 × 15)*
Left	Beacon Street · Corner of Spruce {detail from page 2}	
Opposite	Statue of John Winthrop	
1	Boston skyline {detail from *22.75 × 6* drawing}	
2	Beacon Street · Corner of Spruce	*(8 × 22)*
3	53/52 Beacon Street	*(13.5 × 22)*
4	Beacon Street · Corner of Joy {detail}	
6	Church of the New Jerusalem {detail}	
7	Church of the New Jerusalem	*(28 × 22)*
8	Earle Hotel · Phillips Street {detail}	
9	Looking down Phillips Street	*(28 × 22)*
10–11	Derne Street · Summer afternoon {detail}	
12	Rollins Place	*(15 × 13)*
13	71/69 Hancock Street	*(16 × 20)*
14	Joy Court	*(23 × 37.5)*
15	36$^1/_2$ Joy Court · 3rd floor	*(29 × 23)*
16	Temple Street	*(26 × 23)*
17	Temple Street {detail}	
18	Louisburg Square	*(15 × 20)*
19	Balconies · Louisburg Square {detail}	
20	West End {detail from *11 × 7* drawing}	
21	West End {detail}	
22	Phillips Street/West Cedar {detail from *13 × 16* drawing}	
23	Alley off Joy Street	*(15 × 14)*
24	Parking Lot {composite}	
25	Morgan Memorial · South End	*(12 × 16)*
26	Longwood Avenue near Brookline Avenue {detail}	
27	Longwood Avenue near Brookline Avenue	*(20 × 15)*

28 Life Class · Massachusetts College of Art *(15 × 10)*

29 Drawing Studio · Massachusetts College of Art *(15 × 10)*

30–31 Antique Shop below Charles Street {detail from *20 × 30* drawing}

32 Engineers' Club · Commonwealth Avenue *(23 × 20)*

33 Engineers' Club {detail}

34 175 Newbury Street *(22 × 28)*

35 Jorge's Kiosk {detail}

36 Blockhouse Studio · 175 Newbury Street {detail}

37 Blockhouse Studio · 175 Newbury Street *(30 × 30)*

38 Tower of Abandoned Church · South End {detail}

39 Abandoned Church *(14 × 11)*

40 "No Trespassing" · Roxbury {detail}

41 "No Trespassing" · Roxbury *(11.5 × 14.5)*

42–43 Near Savin Hill · Dorchester *(18 × 14)*

43 Orthodox Church · Chelsea *(13 × 23.5)*

44 Pizzeria · Revere *(23 × 14.25)*

45 Gilmore Motors · East Boston *(11 × 14)*

47 36$\frac{1}{2}$ Joy Court · First Floor *(29 × 23)*

48 Main Street · Stoneham {detail}

49 Main Street · Stoneham *(26 × 18)*

50 Mansion · Marblehead {detail of *12 × 17* drawing}

51 Mansion · Newton Upper Falls *(28 × 22)*

52 House · North Cambridge {detail}

53 Three Houses · North Cambridge *(23 × 14)*

54 Street · Dorchester {detail}

55 Three Decker · Dorchester *(15 × 22)*

56 330 Ash Street · Dorchester *(11 × 14)*

57 Jamaica Plain *(15 × 22)*

Part II   *North and South of Boston*

Drawings and Dimensions (WIDTH AND HEIGHT IN INCHES)

Left	Winter Street · Salem {detail of page 84}
Opposite	North End of Winter Street · Salem {detail of page 92}
58	Peabody · Corner House *(21.5 × 18.25)*
60–61	Ropes Mansion Fence · Salem *(18 × 14)*
62–63	The Oceanside Hotel · Magnolia *(29 × 20.5)*
64–65, 66–67	The Oceanside Hotel · Magnolia {details}
68	The Moorings · Wellfleet *(18 × 14)*
69	The Arbutus · Wellfleet *(16 × 14)*
70	Bradford Street · East end of Provincetown {detail of *16 × 12* drawing}
71	Higgins House · Bound Brook Island, Wellfleet *(16 × 12)*
72	Old Salem Burying Ground {detail}
73	Old Salem Burying Ground *(22 × 15)*
75	41 Washington Square · Salem · Dining room *(22 × 12)*
76	Washington Square · {detail}
77	The Melba · Washington Square · Salem *(30 × 22.5)*
78	Washington Square Fence {detail}
78–79	80 Washington Square · Salem *(21 × 15)*

80–81	Hawthorne Boulevard · Salem *(22 × 12)*
83	Old Custom House · Salem *(21 × 15)*
84–85	Winter Street · Salem *(21 × 15)*
86	Figurehead from "Western Belle" · Peabody Museum · Salem *(6.5 × 9.5)*
87	The Old Salem Hospital · Hawthorne Boulevard *(22 × 13)*
88	Central Salem {detail}
89	Central Salem *(22 × 15)*
90	North End of Winter Street · Salem *(22 × 15)*
91	North End of Winter Street {detail}
92–93	North End of Winter Street · Salem *(22 × 25)*
94–95	Near Collins Cove · Salem *(22 × 15)*
96	Winter Street · Salem {detail}
97	Winter Street at Bridge Street · Salem *(27 × 23)*
98	41 Washington Square {detail}
99	41 Washington Square · Salem · 2nd Floor *(20 × 30)*
100	*Notes on Pens, Inks, and Perspectives*
101	*About the Artist/Author*
Back cover	*Portrait of the Artist by Jack Coughlin*

Part I
A City Upon a Hill

Corner of Beacon at Spruce Street. J. Dumb

On the edge of the Common across from this row of nineteenth century town houses on the slope of Beacon Street that ends by the State House is the Puritan Monument, inviting passers-by to "... consider that we shall be as a city upon a hill and the eyes of all people shall be upon us."

On that Hill I first felt the special excitement of the city where the grassy expanse of Common sweeps down beside Beacon Street to Charles in a panorama of permanence and power. I was entranced by the steep narrow streets lined with intricate brick facades of houses in which interesting things happened long ago, and impressed by the solidity and elegance of brownstone mansions set back from wide avenues in the Back Bay. I was attracted by Newbury Street, where owners of art galleries in converted basements promised fame and fortune for clever art students. I was delighted to find an apartment in an ancient yellow brick house on Joy Street.

Much has changed in Boston. My children who have been there seldom recognize the buildings in my drawings. They photograph each other sitting on a bench next to a bronze statue of James M. Curley across from Quincy Market, where I used to shop for groceries.

In that city I knew many years ago the pace was perhaps slow, the subways dirty, the natives not too friendly, the politicians probably corrupt, but it was an exciting place in which to live and learn and draw.

Across Phillips Street from the State Office Building was the Swedenborgian CHURCH OF THE NEW JERUSALEM, lost sometime in the nineteen sixties to the re-development that swept away most of the eighteenth and nineteenth century buildings on the eastern slope of Beacon Hill.

NEW-JERUSALEM CHURCH

Further down Phillips Street the quiet neighborhood of two and three story apartment houses merged across Cambridge Street into the lively ethnic enclaves of the Old West End where Jewish bakers produced the best bagels north of New York City.

A QUIET SUMMER AFTERNOON ON DERNE STREET... J Doul ... 1953

Derne Street, just below the State House parking lot, was always being repaired. I liked drawing there on hot summer Sundays. In a city deserted by everyone who could get away to a beach there were no vehicles to block my view of street level doors and windows. People who were around often wanted to talk. I kept my big shepherd, "Schopenhauer," close; a good natured beast, he could produce a convincing growl for pushy strangers.

The Doric portico at the end of this Revere Street alley is a truly false facade, hiding nothing but a steep drop off the back side of Beacon Hill.

My friends who lived on the third floor at 71 Hancock Street were only a few minutes walk from any place in central Boston, and it was down hill all the way.

I lived a block away in an ancient yellow brick building at the end of JOY COURT, behind the BEACON CHAMBERS~MEN ONLY. Student housing has never been good in Boston, in my time it was at least cheap. My friend Rusty and I paid twenty dollars a month for our third floor attic studio. We could stand up in almost half the space. The bathroom was on the second floor, only there was no bath. Luckily the fireplace worked, as the furnace often did not.

14

TEMPLE ST.

NO PARKING
ON EITHER SIDE

EXCEPT BY RESIDENTS OF LOUISBURG SQ.
TRESPASSING WILL BE PROSECUTED

Christopher Columbus at one end and Plato at the other still monitor the comings and goings of those Bostonians whose daily routine takes them along the cobblestone lane encircling Louisburg Square, on the side of the Hill that has always been fashionable.

The West End began at the foot of Joy Street. Squeezed between the expansion of the Massachusetts General Hospital complex and transportation corridors around the North Station, it was the first part of Boston to be "re-developed." Scollay Square and the Old Howard Burlesque Theatre disappeared after half-hearted protests. Then I watched whole blocks of old, narrow, brick three and four story tenements knocked down.

I knew that many of these old buildings, squalid after years of neglect by absentee landlords, some of whom actually lived nearby on higher slopes of the Hill, had become dirty, dark, horrible places in which to live. But it was sad to see whole neighborhoods destroyed to make space for parking lots and tourist motels.

I paid sixty dollars for this 1936 green Dodge convertible. The first car I ever owned, it had a rumble seat and, I thought, lots of class.

NEVER TOO POOR
TO PRAY
NEVER TOO WEAK
TO WIN
was the philosophy expressed at the Morgan Memorial in the South End. The POOR fixed things thrown away by the RICH to be sold at the "sheltered workshop", where many of us found pots, chains and other treasures we could afford.

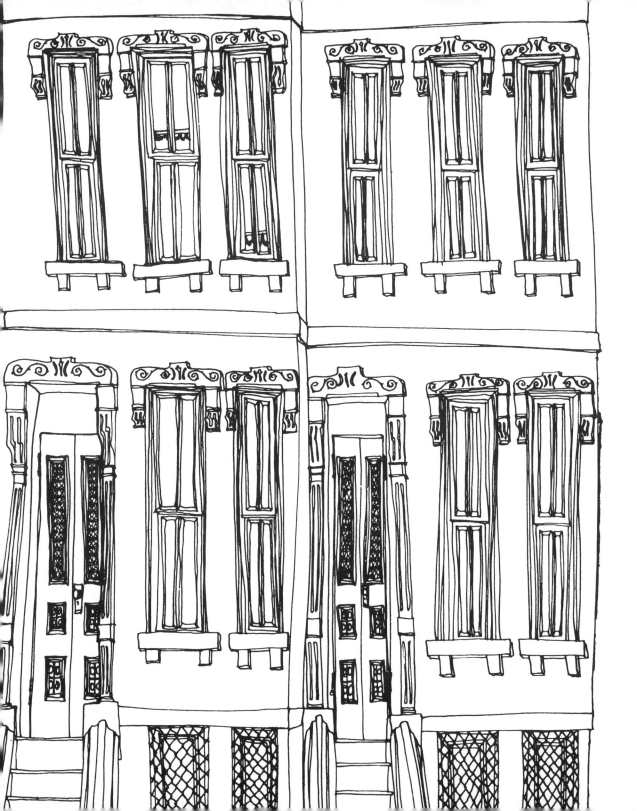

The nineteenth century architect who designed these rowhouses on Longwood Avenue angled the facades so sunlight shone into the front rooms at every season.

The Harvard Medical School·Childrens' Hospital Complex has engulfed this whole area now, although my old school, MASS·ART, is still clinging to the corner at Brookline and Longwood Avenues. It's hard to find the old building crouched under the bulk of Beth Israel Hospital.

I think most classes now meet in the multi-story Tower
Building on Huntington Avenue; closer to the Museum of
Fine Arts, of course.

29

Chunks of sandstone were always falling from the facade of the old Engineers' Club on Commonwealth Avenue.

The newer part of the Ritz Carlton Hotel is there now.

32

Jorge Epstein and his partner Kathy had a collection of wonderfully odd objets d'art packed into the cellar and first floor of their building at 175 Newbury Street. The gold-domed Kiosk had been, so Jorge said, the ticket seller's booth at the nineteen-twenties art-deco Metropolitan Movie Theatre on Tremont Street. In the glass case beside the Kiosk I displayed the hand-blocked fabrics my partner and I printed in our second floor BLOCKHOUSE studio.

Jorge had a large repertoire of tales about his Russian grandfather who fled Czarist troops through freezing Siberian nights in a succession of troikas. Enchanted by these stories, customers would part with alarming amounts of cash for what seemed to me questionable examples of "estate jewelry."

Across the street wily Boris Mirski held forth surrounded by old and new art in his always lively gallery.

The window in my
second floor studio
in Jorge's building
looked out onto the
alley between
Newbury Street and
Commonwealth Avenue.
 A person running
up that alley was
not usually a "jogger."
I saw a shooting
one morning, and
the trash cans
were sometimes
quite interesting.

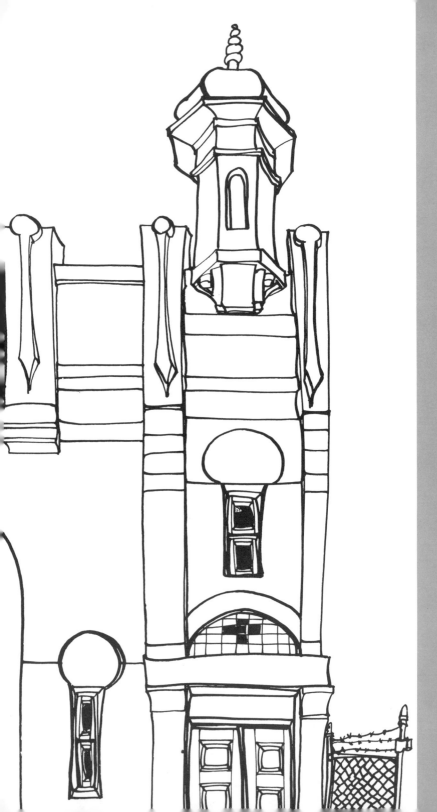

For a while
this abandoned
church in the
South End
was a center
for psychic
activity, a
favorite spot
for convening
the covens.

WILLIAM
COLLINS
CO.
PLUMBING
HEATING

1923

J. Dowl
1955

In Roxbury,
also, there
were
deserted
houses
in semi-
abandoned
neighbor-
hoods

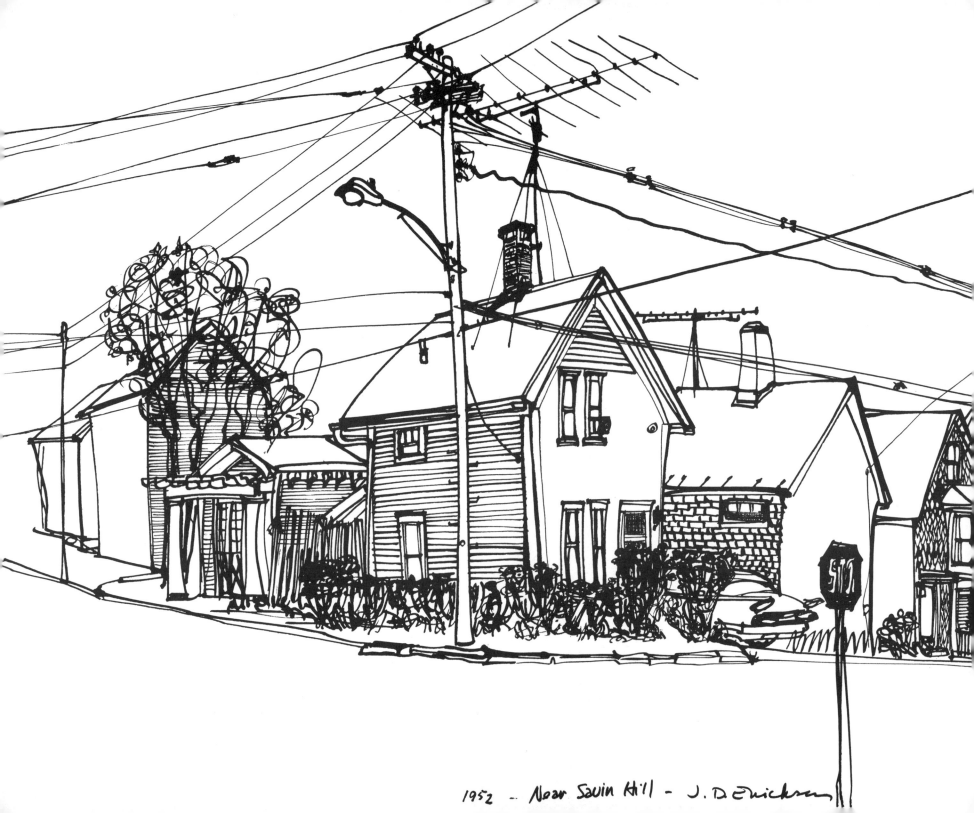

1952 - Near Savin Hill - J. D Erickson

The spires
of this
Orthodox
Church in
Chelsea
gleamed
with
gold leaf
in a
dingy
neigh-
borhood.

Clusters of mysterious structures like this pink stucco pizzeria in Revere spread along the edges of the city. Gilmore Motors was in East Boston, I think.

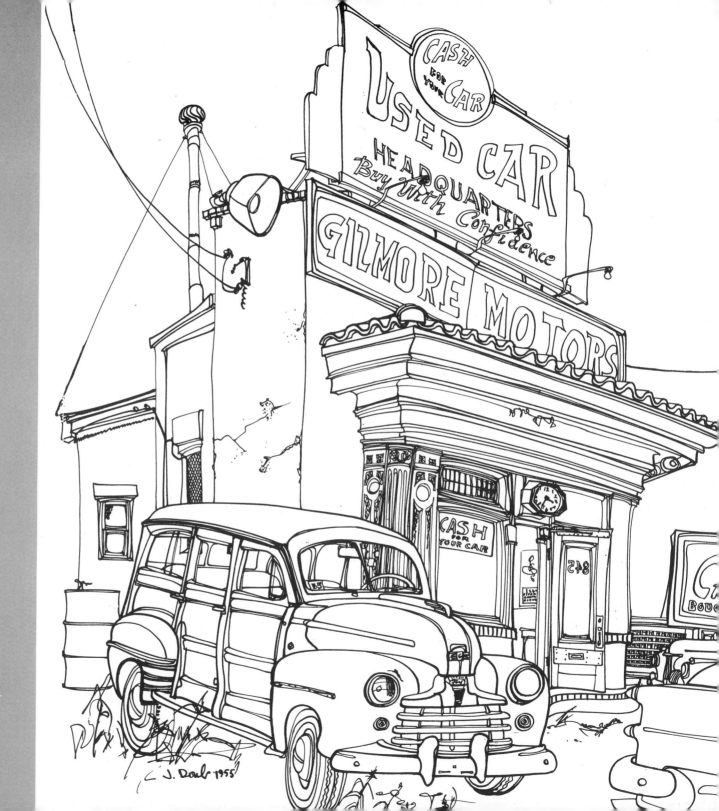

After a while, Schopie and I fell heir to a first floor apartment, with bath and Kitchen, at 36 1/2 Joy Court. As a young man our landlord played the organ in silent movie houses. He installed a huge old pipe organ in the unused stable next door. When the mood was on him he made the basses boom, rattling windows and shaking the building on its ancient foundations.

The Sea Around Us and Other Stories
J. Doudy
1955

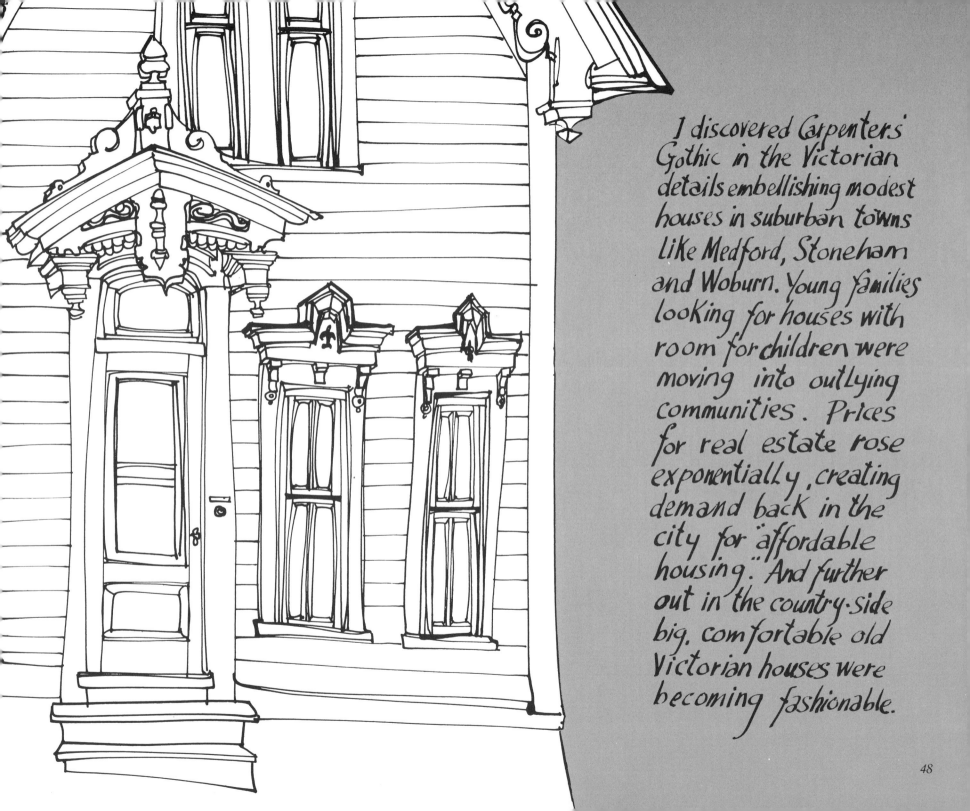

I discovered Carpenters' Gothic in the Victorian details embellishing modest houses in suburban towns like Medford, Stoneham and Woburn. Young families looking for houses with room for children were moving into outlying communities. Prices for real estate rose exponentially, creating demand back in the city for "affordable housing." And further out in the country-side big, comfortable old Victorian houses were becoming fashionable.

Big family homes in this North Cambridge neighborhood were frequently sub-divided to make apartments for students who were coming to the Boston area in increasing numbers every year.

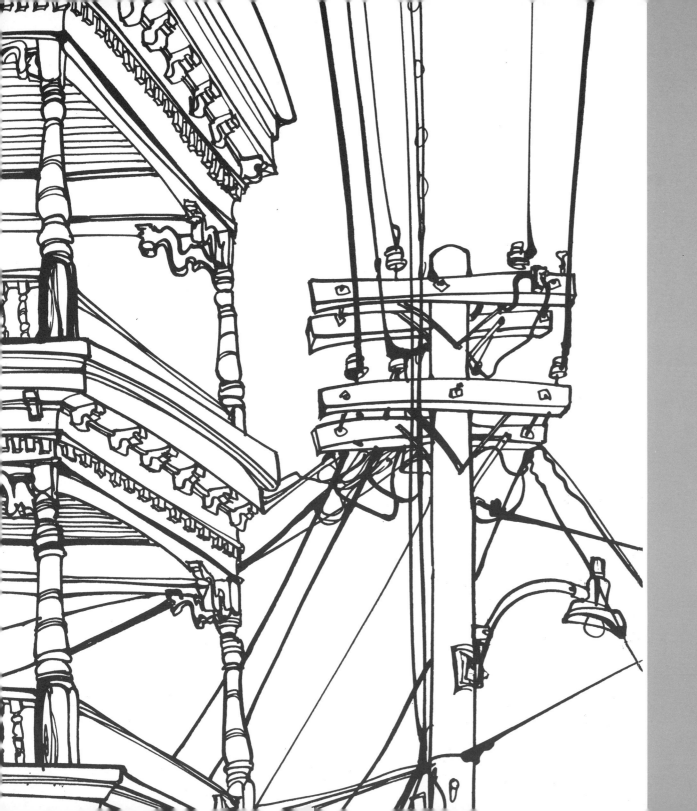

In South Boston, Dorchester, and Jamaica Plain practical "three-deckers" provided comfortable, affordable apartments. Often several generations of one family lived in the same building.

330

L. Doub 1955

56

J.D. ERIKSON

Part II
North and South of Boston

Some superb, and some curious, examples of Yankee craftsmen builders' art on the North Shore and on Cape Cod

The OCEANSIDE hotel at Magnolia, on the coast north of Boston, burned down a long time ago. Fashionable during the early part of the century, by 1947 when I spent a summer there, the long corridors echoed emptily and cats howled from fire-escapes zig-zagging down the land-ward side. A few elderly folk in rocking chairs still sat on the verandas enjoying the splendid view of the Atlantic Ocean. I hoped one of them might buy my drawing, but no one did.

South of Boston, THE MOORINGS in Wellfleet, near the tip of Cape Cod, entertained guests in more modest style.

THE ARBUTUS, I was told, was moved on a
barge from the Methodist Camp Meeting Ground
in Yarmouth to its present site on Holbrook Avenue
by Captain L.D. Baker, whose United
Fruit Company first brought bananas
to New England. He used much of
his considerable fortune to
promote
tourism
on Cape
Cod.

Wellfleet

Long before summer visitors brought Victorian follies to the lower Cape, the Cape Cod Cottage developed a classic form. Derived from traditional fishermen's houses along the windy coasts of western Europe, the compact silhouette and sturdy post and beam construction around a central chimney made it a popular and adaptable style soon seen everywhere along the eastern seaboard.

Higgins House - Bound-Brook Island - Wellfleet

JOHN WATSON PARKER
died Oct 15 1820
aged 21 years

JOHN WATSON
died July 31, 1825
aged 48 years

The Puritans who settled Salem, north of Boston were from a different tradition than that of the fishermen who migrated to Cape Cod and they created for themselves a different society.

The building on the right is the Old Salem jail. Somewhere in the foreground is the place where Peter Corwin was pressed to death for being a witch. "They piled rocks upon his chest untill he was dead."

JOHAN WATSON RIVES
died Oct 15 1620
aged 21 years

JOHN WATSON
died July 31, 1828
aged 48 years

WILLIAM WATSON
son of
JOHN & ABIGAIL WATSON
departed this Life
Sept 2 1823
Aged 82 years

ABIGAIL
wife of
JOHN
died A

J.D. Erickson · 1965

I first knew Salem as the Railway Station where one got off the train from Boston in a huge sooty Gothic structure and took a bus to Marblehead to swim and sail. Later when I moved there with a husband and family of young children, I found a whole town of eighteenth and nineteenth century houses that had survived almost intact into the nineteen · sixties.

We knew that our house on the Common was not really "historic", but it did have lovely spaces and seven working fireplaces. Neighbors were surprised that I was using this corner of the dining room for a studio. They felt the Larkins, who had built the house in 1830, might not approve. In an odd way time was askew in Salem. People spoke of long dead ancestors as they might refer to a relative who had left the room a few minutes ago.

Dispan
1964
J.D.Dickson

This was the view to the left out our front door. The MELBA had been a rooming house for a long time. Beside it Andrews Street led from the Common to the waterfront. Here had been the site of one of the early rope-walks where long strands of hemp were laid straight, then twisted into rope for Salem's sailing ships.

SALEM
J. D. ERICKSON
1966

Members of the
Salem Common
Civic Association
have battled for
years to keep
intact the
wrought iron
pickets fencing
in the eleven
acres of Salem
Common, set
aside in 1714
as a training
field for local
militia.

ONE WAY
DO NOT
ENTER

80

J.P. ERICKSON

J.D. ERICKSON 196

Everyone in Salem knew the story about Nathaniel Hawthorne working as a clerk in the Custom House when he was a poor young writer. When his party lost an election, he lost his job. His wife brought out a bag of money she had saved secretly and said "... now you can write that book." So he did, and The Scarlet Letter became an American classic.

Three blocks from the Custom House, now part of the National Park Service Salem Historic site, the original House of the Seven Gables attracts busloads of tourists all summer long; some of them may even have read Hawthorne's other book, about that odd house.

Salem - 1964

J Erickson · 1966 · WINTER STREET · SALEM

One of the most elegant Greek Revival facades in New England is on Winter Street north of Salem Common. For many years this house at #17 was the parsonage for Old St Peter's Episcopal Church where Tories worshipped, and struggled bitterly with their neighbors who supported Revolutionary ideas held by Sam Adams and others in Boston twenty miles south.

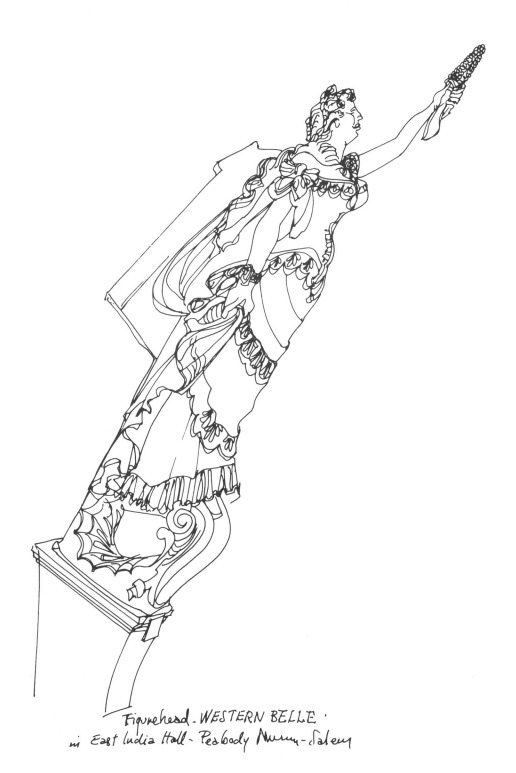

Figurehead - WESTERN BELLE ·
in East India Hall - Peabody Museum - Salem

Salem's wealth came early, brought home by daring young merchant skippers who traded, among other things, ice cut from North Shore ponds, for tea and jade, ivory and fine porcelain, in Canton and Shanghai.

The Old Salem Hospital on Hawthorne Boulevard was founded during this period when money flowed in from the China trade. Later the building became a home for elderly "gentlewomen".

Our central Salem neighborhood was full of eighteenth and nineteenth century houses, although asbestos siding and aluminum skin sometimes hid fine old clapboards and intricate quoins.

Preservationists are now stripping all that off, revealing long concealed architectural details.

Historians are delighted, owners gratified and real estate values enhanced.

SALEM   J.D. ERICKSON 1964

J.D. ERICKSON 1964

This end of
Winter Street
was sald to
have some of
the oldest
structures
remaining
in Salem. I
remember
being told
parts of
this house
had been
dated to
1690.

As fishing and shipping activity took up more space around Salem Harbor people moved out along the North River, building first modest, then grander houses along Essex and Federal Streets.

Across the railroad tracks near Collins Cove houses are not so well preserved, but unusual roof angles and odd window details attract the eyes of architectural historians and sometimes lead to interesting discoveries.

Bob's Market on Bridge Street was the oldest continuously operating grocery in Salem when I shopped there.

Now it's a bike rental agency.

WINTER AND BRIDGE STREETS · SALEM · J.D. ERICKSEN · 1966

The view from my Drawing room at 41 Washington Square in Salem was different from that I now see through a bamboo thicket across fog-blurred towers of Oakland to San Francisco Bay.

The geraniums here grow weedily outside the window instead of inside in pots, but the foreground is still a clutter of pens, ink and brushes. This baby's bottle was abandoned by grandson Sean, rather than by son Lars, but the perspective really hasn't changed much.

1965
41 Washington Sq.
Salem

Notes on Pens, Inks, and Perspectives

Most of these drawings were made using a fine-point, flexible, round-shanked steel pen called "crow quill," dipped in India drawing ink. I like Pelican brand because the top of the bottle can be screwed on tight. Fine pen lines hold up best on very smooth paper. I usually use two- or three-ply Strathmore bristol board or smooth illustration board.

Sometimes I mark a few orientation points lightly in pencil before starting to work in ink, perhaps indicating a tricky roof angle or the complicated relationships of some objects. But I have learned that working out too complete a pencil study makes retracing lines in ink merely tedious — the liveliness and spontaneity of directly translating observation into image is lost forever. And a few "wrong" ink lines can be ignored, or erased with a sharp razor blade if too distracting, when the drawing is complete. (Bend the paper slightly, and a thin clip of paper, with the "wrong" lines, can be sliced from the surface.)

Perspectively, I put myself center front in the drawing, rather than following the late-Renaissance model and chopping out a section of "composition" to frame within the four edges of the paper. I try to think myself out of, and above, the center "station-point" to correct for parallax inevitable in one- and two-point perspective systems. I can keep individual objects in reasonable relationship this way, and can also draw long or tall buildings and panoramas with a sense of accurate proportion, avoiding distortion inherent in conventional architectural renderings. This floating "station point" is also amusing when used to project a feeling of interior space, as in "Third Floor, $36\frac{1}{2}$ Joy Court" on page 15.

Before starting a drawing, I like to walk around and look at details of structure from several angles to isolate unique aspects of place or construction. Then I sit a while, visualizing sizes and scale until the image begins to come clear. Actual drawing seems to take not much time if all goes well. Usually I start with the closest part of a building, person, or object — the roof of a bay window, the top of a pediment, an ear, or the license plate on an automobile bumper — and draw that in completely, finishing each detail before going on to the next so the image develops spatially in sequential layers. I do not make close objects loom large as a camera lens does, so photographs are of no use to me. Anyway, a photograph has very different qualities from a drawing. Even careful architectural studies blur and flatten details that should be seen dimensionally.

It is convenient if a comfortable rock or curbstone is in the right spot, but I have a cleverly folding Italian stool to sit on, and sometimes a strategically located spot for my car makes it possible to sit inside in any weather, in warmth and with music to work by. When I have finished all that should be done from direct observation and everything is laid in — at least one window of every type drawn in completely, doors, brick patterning, siding textures, fences, trees, signs, and other special features studied — I can stop. I will finish the filling-in later, with a fresh eye, a steadier hand, and more patience.

The "fresh eye" is most important, so that one can see clearly the image actually there on the paper, not the one planned in the beginning. Original concept and final drawing are seldom the same, and that's a good thing, I have found.

About the Artist/Author

Many of the buildings shown in *Drawings of Old Boston Houses* have since vanished under the wrecker's ball. Their preservation in these lovingly done drawings reflects Janet Erickson's long affection for Boston's cityscape and the coastal areas of Massachusetts.

A 1947 graduate of the Massachusetts College of Art, Ms. Erickson has been a founder of an arts cooperative on the North Shore, a partner of Blockhouse of Boston, a custom-craft business on Boston's Newbury Street, an assistant professor of art at the State University of New York at Buffalo, and a lifelong enthusiastic teacher once profiled by *Life* magazine.

Ms. Erickson's work has been exhibited in museums in the United States and Europe, and has been acquired for the permanent collections of leading galleries including the Boston Museum of Fine Arts, the Wadsworth Atheneum in Hartford, and the Saudi Royal Commission. She now lives and works in Oakland, California and Wellfleet, Massachusetts.